Contents

The Life Balance Playbook

Seven Steps to the Life You Deserve

By Laura Landau

ISBN 978-0-9964647-0-3

Editor: Christina Dudley, www.yourbestbookforward.com
Author Photographer: Jessica Schubert-Hall

Dedication

To Evan and Paige,

who taught me to care about balance.

Note from the Author

Why am I Writing this Book?

I recently left my corporate career at Microsoft Corporation after sixteen years. It was an amazing journey with a fantastic company. Like many companies, however, Microsoft can be very greedy with your time and energy. And why not? Most companies will gladly take all you will give them. What made my experience somewhat unique is how I made the uber-competitive, corporate environment work for me, not just work for the company.

Along the way, I learned some great lessons about charting my own path, playing by my own rules, and defining success on my terms. I learned to optimize for me and for the important people in my life, not for external expectations, appearances, or competitive urges.

Was it always easy to keep true to my priorities? No way! It required constant vigilance. Did it sometimes mean passing up the juiciest assignments for ones that fit my life goals better? Yep. But I never lost sight of what I value most in life, and I crafted my career to honor those values. These were tradeoffs I was willing to make.

I base this book on the perspective gained from my experience, as well as learnings from my colleagues, friends, and people I have coached and mentored over the years. I have seen the positive impact great life balance has for people as they wear all their hats: employee, parent, partner, volunteer, sister, friend, you name it. I wanted to share some of the tips I collected to help more people optimize their life balance.

My Process

Writing this book has been a three-year journey. It was kicked off by a request from a colleague to do a presentation to her team on work-life balance. I was just getting on a flight and spent the next three hours outlining that presentation, which then became the first rough outline of "the book."

Over the next couple of years, I worked on it between my work and home commitments. I was determined not to ruin my life balance to write a book about it! That would be wrong. In fact, much of the content of this book was written in hour-long increments, as I sat in back of my minivan during various kid activities.

On the home stretch of the writing process, I found myself applying tips from the book to keep me going. My editor called me out on some productive procrastination I was doing (*busted!*). And I am embracing the advice on perfectionism to quit tinkering and just push Print.

Thanks for joining me on this journey. I hope that you find some ways to improve your life balance and build the life you deserve, and maybe even have a little fun along the way.

Laura Landau

Introduction

Are you always running—on the go, but off-balance, due to your hectic schedule? Is your to-do list longer than the Great Wall of China? Does reviewing your calendar for the week ahead make you want to hide under a rock? Do you feel you're doing everything poorly because there isn't enough time to do *anything* well? Are you lacking space in your life for the things that are important to you?

If you answered *Yes* to any of these questions, your life balance needs work and this book is for you! Come along with me to break out of your patterns and find better balance. I know you can do better. You *deserve* to do better. *The Life Balance Playbook* will help you get there.

Busy Bees

When was the last time you asked someone, "How are you?" and the answer wasn't "busy"? Busy, busy, busy. Whatever happened to that quaint reply, "Fine, how are you?" That one was equally useless, in terms of learning anything about the other person, but at least it avoided the passive-aggressive, competitive stance.

"Busy" has become a pathetic badge of honor. "I am sooooo busy." "I worked until midnight last night." "I haven't had dinner with my kids all week." Well, hooray for you.

Please! STOP the busy for busy's sake.

Break the addiction and take control of your life. Get the balance you deserve.

What is Life Balance?

And why "life balance" vs. "work-life balance"? I choose the phrase "life balance" intentionally. Work is part of our lives, not a distinct entity that should get first, or even equal, billing. The term "work-life balance" gives work too much power. *The Life Balance Playbook* is about keeping you in the driver's seat.

Life balance is an ongoing, inexact, opinion-based, purely qualitative measure of how much control you are exercising over your life. It's a feeling. It measures how well you are honoring your priorities and how that makes you feel.

Life balance is something to *optimize* rather than *achieve*, since it's dangerous to think of life balance as a destination with a stopping point.

When you have optimized your life balance, you are honoring each part of your life with the time and attention it deserves, based on your priorities. You are in control.

Want the silver bullet to optimizing your life balance?

Decide what you want, and build your life to make it true.
Make decisions and tradeoffs that best honor your life priorities.

That's it.

However, just because it's simple to say doesn't mean it's easy to do. You'll still have competing priorities. You will still have others vying for your limited time. You'll probably still have too much to do and not enough time to do it in.

Life balance does not need to equal "not busy." But by thoughtfully choosing how to optimize your balance, choosing how you will spend your time, you will be in control. Even if you won't always like the choices you decide to make, you will have the rationale behind it. Through this understanding can come greater acceptance.

Media and society tell us that we are supposed to want it all, do it all, lean in. I've even read a targeted plea to women telling me if I'm not trying to do it all, I'm abandoning the paths pioneered by our mothers and grandmothers. Oh, yeah? I think that's a load of hooey. We can do better. We owe it to ourselves to make the tough choices to build the lives *we* want. Designing and living the life you want is what makes life balance.

The hard truth: you can't have it all right now. Time is sequential and finite. We all only get twenty-four hours a day.

If you disagree – great! I applaud you for knowing what works for you. Choose a different road to reach the life you want. But know that this book was not written for you. (Although you can definitely glean some good tips.)

This book is for people who are saying, "Hey, wait! The do-it-all-right-now path I'm on no longer works for me. I want something different. I want to decide what *I* want."

Deep Thoughts about the Universe:

I was chatting with my twelve-year-old son, expressing the common mom lament of "I can't believe how old you're getting!"

His response: "It annoys me when people express surprise over the passage of time. It is literally the most predictable thing in the universe."

So true. So true.

Here's What You Will Get

By reading this book and thoughtfully completing the exercises, you will discover *you* have the power to improve your life balance. You will get tools and strategies to take your current life, right now, and make decisions and tradeoffs that bring you more balance.

What *The Life Balance Playbook* will help you do:

- Figure out your most important priorities.
- Determine what success looks like for you.
- Figure out some balance problem-spots and opportunities.
- Look at your own behaviors and those around you.

What *The Life Balance Playbook* will NOT do for you:

- Make your life easy.
- Teach you how to have it all.
- Tell you to lean in to your career.

If that's what you're looking for, you'll find other books out there dangling those promises.

You deserve better life balance. I want to help you optimize your life balance and make your life work for you! That is the goal of *The Life Balance Playbook*.

Michelle's Story:

Michelle was in a horrific car accident that nearly killed her. For real. Before it happened, she had already started down the path of making tradeoffs to build the life she loved – but that experience reinforced her commitment. She has healed, but as with many survivors of tragedies, she points to it as a defining moment in her life.

I want to help you transform your life, but let you skip the near-death experience! You can choose from where you are right now. No tragic trigger required.

How to Use This Book

Here are some of things you'll need to do, to be successful on this journey:

- Be honest with yourself.
- Let go of the guilt.
- Challenge your assumptions.

Each chapter will share a concept and give you a checklist, so you will know exactly what you should accomplish in that chapter. You'll also find Deep Thoughts, pieces of information relevant but tangential to the topic, and stories to illustrate the points, both from my own life as well as others' (If these bore or annoy you, just skip them.).

The most important parts of the book are the exercises. As you encounter them, try not to get impatient. *I know and respect that you are busy.* The exercises are important to complete thoughtfully to be able to apply the concepts to *your* life.

Some of the exercises may make you uncomfortable, which is a good thing! They are designed to help you break out of the pain cave you're in today and look to a better future.

I intentionally keep this book as short as possible. But if you get bogged down, don't abandon. Keep reading and circle back to complete the exercises. (The chapters get less introspective as you move through them.)

Go ahead, bend the corners of pages, write in the book, use sticky notes—or, if you like your books to remain pristine, download Exercise Worksheets from www.lifebalanceplaybook.com.

Commit to change

Do you want to improve your life balance? Really? As in, *really* really? The biggest impact on your life balance will be your commitment to change.

Rate yourself on a scale of 1-5. How committed are you to making changes to improve your life balance?

5: This is it! I'm ready to take back control and will stop at nothing.

4: I really want this, I want to find some strategies that will help.

3: Life balance would be great. I'll look for a few small places to start.

2: HA! This is wishful thinking. But I'll mark some ideas for later, when it seems more feasible.

1: My friend gave me this book, so I'll flip through it to please them.

Commitment Rating: _____

Warning! Resistance Ahead!

As you work through the playbook and exercises, prepare to meet resistance. This might come from others, but your biggest resistance will come from your own, internal voice. You know, that running commentary inside your head that tells you you're not good enough, that you don't deserve better, or asks, "Who do you think you are?" And let's not forget one of my favorites—*I cannot believe you just did that!*

This voice has been called the inner voice, gremlin or even itty-bitty-committee. I'll call this voice your "saboteur," since it is when this voice is negative that it does the most damage to your life balance. (I will also call the saboteur "she" for simplicity, not to make a political statement.)

To change your life and optimize your life balance, you need to control this little voice. This voice will tell you to cling to your bad habits, even though they no longer work for you, and will call it safety.

Tips on identifying input from your saboteur:

- Any negative self-talk.
- You say or think, "I should…"
- You neutralize a bold, positive statement by following it with a downer.

A few more things to know about your saboteur:
- Your saboteur is very clever, so you will need to be on guard constantly for her influence.
- She will try hardest to keep you from the things you truly want the most.

I'll cover specific tactics to deal with your saboteur later in the book.

Now, with the warning issued, let's move on to the good stuff.

Let's Take a Tour of the Playbook

The *Life Balance Playbook* is broken into seven steps. They range from introspective and challenging to simple, straightforward, and a maybe even a little bossy. Work through these steps in order and you'll be on your way to improving your life balance.

Let's define each step at the 10,000-foot level:

DESIGN the life you want. Define the building blocks of your life balance and imagine what is possible.

DIAGNOSE where you are today. Evaluate your current state.

DEAL with yourself. The biggest threat to life balance is….you. Take a look in the mirror and figure out what to do.

DETERMINE the role of others. As the star and director of your life, you get to define the roles that others play.

DECIDE smarter. Explore tradeoffs you are making and how you are deciding.

DO what it takes. Learn efficiency tips in this straightforward section.

DEFEND your progress. Set yourself up for long-term success.

Got it? Sound good to you?

Then let's get started!

DESIGN the Life You Want

Before heading out on a trip, we usually have a destination in mind. Some people make very specific plans on how to get there; they've printed the directions and reviewed the route. Others just grab their phone (or a map, if they're old school or practicing orienteering) and head out the door. But either way, we know where we want to go.

In this chapter, you will be looking at your priorities and how you define success. These findings will serve as the North Star for your life. When you are lost, you can refer back to these to remind you what is most important.

What does this have to do with life balance? Everything.

Knowing what you *want* builds the foundation for the decisions and tradeoffs you need make to optimize your life balance. Design your life, so you will be able to make the right choices to get there or even partway there.

Disclosure: I get impatient with people who are unhappy with what they have, but can't articulate what they *do* want. You know, those people who can only complain about what it is, or is not, at that moment. My view is, if you don't know what you want, how can you complain about not having it?

To figure out what we really want, it helps to give ourselves permission to adopt a certain mindset. Just for this chapter, try this one on for size:

- Ignore your current reality, and turn off the "yes, but..." in your head.

By the end of this chapter you will have:

1. Prioritized aspects of your life.
2. Defined success.
3. Built your dream calendar.

Tell Me What You Want, What You Really, Really Want

The first step to improve your life balance is to understand what is most important to you. You might be thinking – wait a minute – I thought this book would tell me what to do! Yes and no. You will have to do the work to get the answers that will work for you. You are the expert on your life.

So much of our life feels prescribed, it can be hard to articulate what we want. The following are a couple of exercises to get you started on defining your best life.

Page from My Playbook:

Luther College, Decorah, IA: I was interviewing for my first post-college job at a large financial services firm. The company had sent one of their shiny up-and-comers to campus to find the next generation of talent (me, of course!). I was dressed in my conquer-the-business-world armor: power suit, silk blouse, black pumps, and even pantyhose. I had printed my resume on textured ecru paper and was ready to impress. I had an extra copy tucked into my leatherette folder which held a fresh legal pad. I knew I was perfect for their job. Just wait until they learned more about me and my fabulousness!

The interview was going fine until the recruiter did a confusing thing. He asked me what I wanted in a job.

Panic ensued. What I wanted in a job? What *I* wanted? My dream job was what they needed, what they were recruiting for, ummm, what was that again? They had been vague in the job description.

From there, the interview went downhill fast. I so wish I had said, "Clearly this is not going well. Why don't you take a break until your next interview?" Needless to say, my glorious future in the financial industry ended there.

Exercise: Life Priorities – Part 1

Your life is comprised of many facets, and each person will value and allocate their time and energy differently. In this exercise, you will take a look at the various parts of your life and decide which are most important.

As you complete this exercise, be honest and do not judge yourself. This is not the place for "I should" or internal or external peer pressure. Watch out for your saboteur.

Step 1:   Using the list below, decide what is most important. Circle the 8-10 most important. Feel free to add or combine categories to better reflect what is important to you.

Some common priorities include:

Adventure	Learning	Romance
Career	Mentoring	Sleep
Creativity	Money – Security	Spirituality
Family	Money - Status	Travel
Friends	Recreation	Volunteering
Health/Exercise		

Now transfer your list of top life priorities to the table below.

Life Priority	Importance

Step 2:   For each, rate its <u>importance</u> to you on a scale of 1-10.

Step 3:   Circle or highlight anything that scores over a 7 in importance.

Any surprises? Did anything score higher than you imagined? Lower?

Congratulations! You have just completed your first step in designing the life you want. And if someone asks you what you gives your life meaning, you now have an idea!

Imagine your Future

Now that you identified your priorities, the next exercises will help define what you want your future to be.

Start with Exercise 1: Future Self, and then choose one or more variations of Exercise 2: Magazine Article, Obituary, or Party Guest. Then, wrap up the section with a nostalgic visit to your happiest Past Self in Exercise 3.

Exercise 1: Future Self

Talking to your future self is a great way to identify what is most important to you. This a twist on the "Dear 16-year-old me" video, books and blogs you may have seen.

When we're young, it's hard to listen to the hard-earned advice of those who have come before us. And, as a not-as-young-as-I-used-to-be person, I often get frustrated with young people who aren't open to my most excellent advice. The Future Self exercise bridges these together. You will be giving yourself advice.

If you're a very logical person, this exercise might feel awkward. Remember, discomfort is good! It will help you see things from a new perspective. Embrace it.

First, go somewhere quiet for this exercise. Get comfortable and relax. You will want to close your eyes to imagine your future self. If you have a coach or trusted friend, this can be a great exercise to enlist their help to ask you the questions. But only do this if you won't then filter your responses.

Step 1:   Pick a time horizon in the future at least ten years out. I like fifteen years when I do this – it's removed enough from my current reality, but not too far.

Step 2: Imagine yourself as your future self. Visualize it. Think about your other senses as well. Be specific. Answer the following questions to help you describe your future self.

How old are you?	
How old are your family members?	
Where do you live?	
Who lives with you?	
What does your house look like?	
How are you dressed?	
What do you see? What do you smell?	
What do you plan to do today?	
What do you value most in your life right now?	
What are you most proud of?	
How do you want to be remembered?	

Now reflect on the exercise.

What did you notice about the Future Self you pictured?

What would your Future Self say to you right now?

Amy's Story:

Amy is successful career woman with an urban vibe and fashionista flair. In her mid-thirties, she found herself single, living in the suburbs to be close to work, and working 10-12 hours a day.

She then did the Future Self exercise. What she imagined was dramatically different from where she was. Her future self was living in the city, with a family, and spending less time at work. By drawing this picture, she knew she needed to make some big changes to get aligned with where she wanted to be.

Five years later, she has a lovely adopted daughter, a growing, successful business, and a schedule that she controls. She is surrounded by her tribe in an city neighborhood. No more 'burbs for Amy!

Now, choose from the following exercises.

Exercise 2A: Magazine Article

For this exercise, imagine twenty years have passed. You have just published an article in a magazine. You'll get to decide who it is written for, what magazine it's in and the title.

Make sure and tell your saboteur to be quiet! You have something to say and the world deserves to hear it!

Now, write a short paragraph describing the author (that would be you). Describe yourself in glowing terms. If it's challenging to describe yourself in glowing terms, pretend you're talking about someone else. Write her bio. Don't worry, she won't mind.

Page from My Playbook:

I did a similar exercise for a class about five years ago, where I was challenged to describe a book I would write. Here's what I came up with. The intended audience was professional working women.

Having Half of it All: One Woman's Part-Time Journey Through Corporate America. Meet author Laura Landau, who has spent 10+ years in one of the most fast-paced industries at one of the most competitive companies in America today—Microsoft. By carving her own path against all odds, she has been able to work part-time, while still earning promotions and awards.

I never actually wrote the book, but putting it on paper inspired me to continue to march to my own drummer and not let others define success for me. And it also put out there in the universe my desire to write a book for real. This book is the v.2 of that vision.

Now, it's your turn.

Audience:
Title:
Magazine:
Your Bio:

Exercise 2B: Obituary

As a person who seeks the positive in my life, this is not my favorite exercise, but it works for many. Imagine you've come to the end of your long life. Write your obituary, detailing your life's accomplishments and legacy.

Obituary:

Exercise 2C: Guest of Honor

Imagine you're the guest of honor at a party with fabulous people. What is your story? Let your imagination run free. No limits, no saboteur. Write the host's introduction for you to the group, before you stand up to share your short and pithy remarks.

Page from My Playbook:

Let me introduce Laura Landau. She is the author of *The Life Balance Playbook*, which has helped launch a global phenomenon of people taking control of their lives and creating lives that optimize their life balance by making tradeoffs that honor their priorities. People are living with more calm and more joy than ever before.

Following her last appearance on the *Ellen* show (make sure and ask her about sharing the green room with Ryan Gosling), she was awarded Person of the Year by *Time* and *Working Mother* magazines.

She is widely credited with the falling rate of anti-anxiety prescriptions in the US. Studies have linked it back to the calm and balance individuals are building for themselves, using the lessons from the *Playbook*.

It's fun to share your faux awesomeness. Try it!

Guest of Honor Introduction:

Now, we'll take a moment to look backwards to find some clues about what you value most in your life.

Exercise 3: Glory Days

Think about a point in time when things just felt right. A time when you were most content with your life, job, etc. You were really in the groove.

Pick a moment in time and describe what you were doing and how you felt; be specific and use all your senses. This will offer some clues into things you value.

Page from My Playbook:

I did this exercise several years ago, and one particular moment came very clearly into my head. I was doing a puzzle with my son, singing along to the Weird Al Yankovic *Star Wars* parody (don't judge – it's clever), my daughter was dancing along in a diaper and princess shoes, and a warm breeze was coming in from outside on lovely summer day.

I then reflected on this moment and why it was so pivotal. I realized that I was *fully* present in that moment, in a way that I often was not when spending time with my kids. No to-do lists running in head, no sneak peeks at email, nothing on the stove.

From this, I decided to try harder to focus on being 100% where I was, whether at home or at work.

Describe your moment.

Why does it stand out for you?

Exercise: Wrap-Up

Reflect on the previous exercises.

What did you learn from these exercises?

What will you use to help you design your life?

Revisit your life priorities. Is there anything you'd like to change? Feel free. After all, it's your life.

Next, Define Success

Success. Peddled by inspirational speakers and high school cheerleaders (S-U-C-C-E-S-S!), everyone wants it, but most people wouldn't agree on what it means. Even fewer have taken the time to think about how they would define success for themselves.

Is it money? Prestige? Accolades? Close connection to those you love? Significance, in the scheme of things? Like life balance, success is very personal. You need to define it for yourself. If not defined correctly and customized for you, using "success" as a goal can do more harm than good.

Page from My Playbook:

For me – being balanced is one of things I use to define success in my life. I want to have an interesting and challenging career, enough money for a comfortable life, a strong marriage, and to raise two kids to the best of my ability. I also want to have time to volunteer, time to spend with friends and family, and time to read, exercise and just chill.

To help me keep the big picture in mind at work, I define success as follows: do interesting work that matters (keep learning and add value); get rewarded for what I do (make money); work with great people (have fun); have flexibility (see my family and enjoy my life).

As you can see, my career success and life success are interrelated. My work success is a part of my life success, but it's not the only thing that defines success for me.

Deep Thoughts about Resumes:

Build your life, not your resume.

Exercise: Define Success

Answer the following questions, building on your work in the previous exercises. Take time to be introspective here. Really, truly, at the end of your life, what do you want to have accomplished? What kind of life do you want to live as you journey to get there?

Think holistically. Think beyond career and work success. If it is helpful, do a separate definition for your career on the following page.

How you define success for your life long term?

How do you define success for your current stage of life?

Circle back to your Future Self. Does she have any thoughts on success for your life?

Exercise: Career Success (optional)

If helpful, spell out your career success as well. As you think about this, try to avoid specific goals like "become a VP by forty." Translated to a higher level, that could be "achieve status and responsibility."

How do you define career success long term?

How you define career success for your current stage of life?

How do your career success criteria support your life success criteria?

Build a Dream Calendar

If you're like me, your life is driven by your calendar. If it's on the calendar, it's likely to happen. If it's not on the calendar, it doesn't exist.

Exercise: Your Ideal Week

In the next exercise, you get to have some fun. You will fill in a calendar that looks exactly how you'd like it to.

As you complete this exercise, remember this is your ideal calendar. Be greedy. Imagine the ideal life in a typical week (doing a vacation week is cheating). Forget your real calendar for a minute or two. What would your dream calendar look like? Block time for what you want. Ask for the moon here, or even the moon and back.

Step 1:   Define your day: What time will get up? What time will you go to bed? That's the number of waking hours you'll have to work with. Do not include any early morning insomnia hours – these do NOT count.

Step 2:   Details: Assign the blocks of time. These should align to your priorities – even if you use more specific details here. Include "Open" time as well.

Here is an example in black and white, but if you visualize better with color coding, be my guest!

	Sun	Mon	Tues	Wed	Thurs	Fri	Sat
12:00am -4:00							
4:00-5:00				Sleep			
5:00 – 6:00							
6:00 – 7:00							
7:00 – 8:00	Sleep			Breakfast			
8:00 – 9:00	Bfast	Yoga		Tennis		Yoga	Tennis
9:00 – 10:00	Open	Open		Open		Open	
10:00 – 11:00	Church			Volun-			Open
11:00 – Noon			Work	teer	Work		
Noon – 1:00		Work				Work	
1:00 – 2:00				Friend			Family
2:00 – 3:00	Family			Open			
3:00 – 4:00			Open				
4:00 – 5:00			Kids				Open
5:00-6:00	Friends						Kids
6:00 – 7:00			Dinner			Open	
7:00 – 8:00			Walk				
8:00 – 9:00	Open		Open			Date	Friends
9:00 – 10:00							
10:00 – 11:00			Read				
11:00 – 12:00			Sleep				

If this calendar makes you jealous...good. It's a dream calendar. Now your turn.

Your Dream Calendar

Now you try on the following page.

When you are done, take a minute to revel in this amazing week. If you don't love it – keep working on it until you do.

High five! You have now completed the design phase and we move on to diagnose your current situation.

	Sun	Mon	Tues	Wed	Thurs	Fri	Sat
12:00am -4:00							
4:00-5:00							
5:00 – 6:00							
6:00 – 7:00							
7:00 – 8:00							
8:00 – 9:00							
9:00 – 10:00							
10:00 – 11:00							
11:00 – Noon							
Noon – 1:00							
1:00 – 2:00							
2:00 – 3:00							
3:00 – 4:00							
4:00 – 5:00							
5:00-6:00							
6:00 – 7:00							
7:00 – 8:00							
8:00 – 9:00							
9:00 – 10:00							
10:00 – 11:00							
11:00 – 12:00							

DIAGNOSE Where You Are

When you get sick, you just want to feel better. Whether you go to the doctor, check with Google, or call your mom, the first step is to get a correct diagnosis. For life balance, there is no WebMD. In the Diagnose chapter, you will take a closer look at your current state and try to determine some causes of your less than ideal life balance.

Just as in the first chapter, a particular mindset will help you in the Diagnose phase. This time around make sure to:

- Be honest with yourself, say what you really feel.
- Listen to your initial response, it's often right.

Here's what we are going to do in this chapter:

1. Evaluate your satisfaction with your life priorities.
2. Align your priorities and success measures.
3. Compare your reality and dream calendars.

Determine your Life Balance Baseline

People will often say they're too stressed, which is probably true. They say, "My life balance (or work-life balance) is terrible." Also probably true. But what exactly do these statements mean?

If you've said either of these statements recently, let's try unscientifically to quantify how stressed-out and out-of-balance you really are.

Rate your current stress and life balance levels below. Look at, say, the last two typical weeks to make this evaluation.

Exercise: Stress and Balance

For the following questions, rate on a scale of 1-5.

Stress

Use the following as a guide or use your own scale, when thinking about your stress.

1   Things are great! Refresh my piña colada, would you?

2   I am busy, but am fairly in control (most of the time.)

3   About half the time I feel fine.

4   My life it nuts! Once I unclench my teeth, I'll tell you about it.

5   DEFCON 5. I am about to blow!

What is your current stress level?	
What is your ideal stress level?	
Opportunity (current – ideal)	

Balance

Again, use the following as a guide or use your own, this time thinking about your life balance.

1   Things are great! I feel perfectly satisfied with how I allocate my time.

2   Generally I spend my time where I like, with occasional exceptions.

3   At least 50% of the time I am satisfied with where my time goes.

4   Too often lower life priorities crowd out what I'd rather be doing!

5   Ha! All my time is going where I don't want to spend it!!

Rate your life balance	
What is your ideal life balance rating	
Opportunity (current – ideal)	

Now add your two opportunity scores together. _____

Here's what I recommend based on your score.

0   Give this book to a friend who needs it.

2   Have fun with the book. Grab some tidbits.

4   You are within striking distance of your ideal. Look for some key tweaks to get you closer to your goal.

6 Definitely have room for improvement. Roll up your sleeves, and get to work.

8+ YIKES! Big changes are needed. FAST. Make this a priority.

As a reminder, write the commitment rating you declared in the Introduction chapter below. This will remind yourself how badly you want to change.

Commitment Rating: _____

What's Going Well?

It's easy to focus on what's wrong, and forget that oftentimes we are doing quite a few things right. Take a minute to focus on the positive.

In your life today, what feels good and in control? What areas of your life are you currently optimizing effectively? (Come on, there has got to be something!)

Good job celebrating. Now let's revisit your life priorities and how well you're aligning your life against these priorities today.

Exercise: Life Priorities – Part 2

In this exercise, you'll compare the importance of your priorities with your satisfaction level in how well you honor them.

Step 1: Copy the list of your top 8-10 priorities from the Design chapter. List them in order, from most important to least, based on your rating. Include the importance rating assigned.

Step 2: Now, for each priority, rate how satisfied you are with how well you are honoring that aspect of your life.

Step 3: Calculate the difference between importance and satisfaction to identify which are most misaligned.

Step 4: Check back with your Success Criteria. Are the priorities supported by your success criteria?

Example: Life Priorities

Priority	Importance	Current Satisfaction	Importance – Satisfaction (Δ)	Part of success criteria?
Work	7	9	+2	Yes
Romance	8	5	-3	Sort of
Health/Exercise	6	2	-4	No
Family	8	8	0	Yes

Now your turn.

Priority	Importance	Current Satisfaction	Importance – Sat. (Δ)	Success criteria?

Damage Report

Let's take a look at what all this means.

Which priorities have the highest difference between importance and satisfaction?

Which priorities, if any, are not supported by your success criteria?

How does this show up in your life?

This where the hard work kicks in: to align your priorities and success criteria until they are acceptable for you. This doesn't mean they have to be in perfect lockstep; however the closer they are, the more clarity you'll have to design and build the life you want, with more life balance and less stress.

Take a moment to review your priorities and success criteria. Make any adjustments you'd like.

Calendar Comparison

In the next exercise, you'll take a look at the facts of your current calendar.

Exercise: Real Calendar

Step 1: Fill in the calendar template from a typical week in your life. If you used color codes in the Design chapter, use those same codes here.

Step 2: Now compare your real calendar to your dream calendar.

Example: Real Calendar

	Sun	Mon	Tues	Wed	Thurs	Fri	Sat
12:00am -4:00				Sleep			
4:00-5:00							
5:00 – 6:00							
6:00 – 7:00	Sleep			Breakfast			
7:00 – 8:00				Kids/Driving			
8:00 – 9:00	Bfast						Tennis
9:00 – 10:00	Open						
10:00 – 11:00	Church						Errands
11:00 – Noon							
Noon – 1:00	Lunch	Work					Lunch
1:00 – 2:00	Errands /Family						
2:00 – 3:00							Errands/ Family
3:00 – 4:00							
4:00 – 5:00							Open
5:00-6:00	Friends	Soccer	Music	Bball	Soccer	Open	Kids
6:00 – 7:00	Dinner		Dinner			Driving	Open
7:00 – 8:00	Kids		Kids/Homework				Friends/ Date
8:00 – 9:00	Work						
9:00 – 10:00			Work			TV	
10:00 – 11:00							
11:00 – 12:00			Sleep				

Now it's your turn.

	Sun	Mon	Tues	Wed	Thurs	Fri	Sat
12:00am -4:00							
4:00-5:00							
5:00 – 6:00							
6:00 – 7:00							
7:00 – 8:00							
8:00 – 9:00							
9:00 – 10:00							
10:00 – 11:00							
11:00 – Noon							
Noon – 1:00							
1:00 – 2:00							
2:00 – 3:00							
3:00 – 4:00							
4:00 – 5:00							
5:00-6:00							
6:00 – 7:00							
7:00 – 8:00							
8:00 – 9:00							
9:00 – 10:00							
10:00 – 11:00							
11:00 – 12:00							

Circle the areas that are the most different from your Dream Calendar. Going back to the doctor analogy – where does it hurt?

Think about what this means.

Where are you investing more time than your dream calendar?

Where are you doing less?

Are some categories entirely missing on your real calendar?

How well does your reality calendar align with your priorities?

This exercise was designed to pinpoint some specific areas (and provide evidence) where your life balance is not optimized.

Summarize

Look back through this chapter to summarize the diagnosis.

Where, exactly, is your life balance out of whack?

As you continue with the playbook and exercises, keep your key learnings from this chapter in mind.

It will help you prioritize and made tradeoffs you'll need to do to optimize your life balance.

DEAL with Yourself

When thinking about your life balance, you may be tempted to blame work, kids, family, or community commitments. But remember, the only thing these have in common is—you guessed it—you!

It's your life. You need to design and build your life balance. You need to own it. No one can do it for you. So let's do it!

This chapter's mindset:

- Be ready for hard truths about yourself.
- Be open to change.

In this chapter, you will accomplish the following.

- Recognize and deal with your saboteur.
- Identify some unhelpful personas you may take on.
- Learn tips to control these alter egos.

Let's start with the big one!

The Saboteur

You learned about the saboteur in the Introduction. You were warned of potential internal resistance you may face as you attempt to own your life balance and work to improve it. Have you heard from her yet?

To review, your saboteur is the little voice in your head that provides a running commentary of negative self-talk as you live your life. Your saboteur has likely has been active in your life for a long time. Listening to her is a habit and can be a hard one to break.

However, to improve your life balance, you will need to control this voice. This is not optional. In fact, if you talked to a friend the way you sometimes talk to yourself, you would (or should) fire that friend! Who needs it?

Right now, what is your saboteur saying to you? ("Yes, but..." or "Don't listen! This is hooey!" might be a theme.)

Excuses, Excuses

Here are some excuses from the saboteur's greatest hits.

Your saboteur's spin on things	Reality check
"I should be able to do everything, look at [insert name of your always put-together friend/colleague]."	Good for her, but remember, appearances can be deceiving. And really, how is that relevant?
"I don't want to complain. My life is actually pretty good."	It's great to acknowledge what is going right, but it's also okay to target things that could be better.
"I am supposed to be able to do everything."	Says who? What the heck do they know?
[Insert your favorite excuse...]	What is that costing you?

Exercise: Rate your Saboteur

How powerful is your saboteur? Rate the following, using a 1-5 scale.

1 = Not a problem.

5 = My saboteur has super powers. ("Really, is that the best you can do?")

Your saboteur power rating: _____

Let's take a look at the impact your saboteur has on you.

What does your saboteur say to you?

What impact does your saboteur have on your life balance?

What would you like to say to your saboteur?

Another tricky thing about the saboteur is that she plays well with friends. When we fall into the following personas described below, the saboteur often comes along for the ride and provides a cheering section.

The Perfectionist

You know the perfectionist. Nothing is ever good enough. It could be the hypercritical co-worker who, when you proudly present an awesome piece of work, helpfully points out the two words that are in a font two points smaller than the rest of the text. Or perhaps it's the friend who cleans up your coffee cup when you step away to the bathroom . . . in your own house.

Perfectionism isn't always this extreme and does have its pluses, but think about yourself. Is this you?

Deep Thoughts by Voltaire:

In the 1700s, Voltaire tackled this subject in his poem *"La Bégueule"*:

> *Dans ses écrits, un sage Italien,*
> *Dit que le mieux est l'ennemi du bien.*

> *(In his writings, a wise Italian/*
> *Says that the better is the enemy of the good.)*

(Who knew my book would be so lofty!)

Here are a just few of the ways the perfectionist can get you into trouble.

Diminishing Marginal Returns

This is when additional effort doesn't make it any better. At work this can mean checking and rechecking (and rechecking) to make sure everything is exactly right, getting feedback, and more feedback, etc. Did that extra hour (or day, or week) you spent really drive better business results?

Closely related is the 80/20 rule. No, not *that* 80/20 rule, where 20% of the people do 80% of the work (although that could be a problem for you, too). The 80/20 rule for perfectionists states that it takes 20% of the time and effort to complete 80% of a task, while the last 20% of a task takes 80% of the effort.

Analysis Paralysis

"If I only had more info...that last piece of data, I could make a great decision." Analysis paralysis can hit when making a decision at work, making a purchase, or even deciding what's for dinner (you know, when you ask the wait-staff fifteen questions about the preparation).

Do we really need to read every last review to know which blender to buy? I'm not saying information is bad, but it can definitely slow us down and get in our way of making progress. And with unlimited information a click away, this is an easy trap to fall into.

You will *never* have full information, even you if you have unlimited time and money to collect it. Get over it.

Page from My Playbook:

My daughter was nine and obsessed with horses. For Christmas, she wanted an alarm clock. So, like the overindulgent mother that I am, I went straight to Amazon.com and searched on "horse alarm clocks." It might surprise you (or maybe not), but there was more than one option.

I found myself not only looking at the overall star ratings (reasonable amount to research for a $12 purchase in my book), but actually reading all the reviews. Every last one. *Oh my, someone who bought this in 2011 had a bad experience. What should I do? Do I risk it? Could be a lemon...*

I finally shook myself out of it and decided to take the plunge. Because, really, at the end of the day – it didn't really matter, and it was definitely not worth the time I was spending.

> (For the record, I wake every morning now to *clop-clop-clop-clop-whinny-clop-clop-clop-clop-whinny* through the wall. Five stars!)

I am not recommending you let your work get sloppy or that you make snap decisions about important things. But watch for perfectionism that can get in the way of your life balance. And look out for your saboteur here. She thinks perfectionists are awesome!

Excuses, Excuses

Do any of these sound familiar?

From the perfectionist peanut gallery	Reality check
"My work is a reflection of me. It needs to be perfect."	Is there a level of quality short of perfection that's still high quality? Does the extra effort add value?
"My boss/company/spouse sets the bar really high.	Are you setting the bar even higher than they would? What is the cost?
[Insert your favorite excuse ....]	What is that costing you?

Exercise: Rate your Perfectionist

How powerful is your perfectionist? Rate the following using a 1-5 scale.

    1 = Not a problem.

    5 = That's me! (Do I see a smudge on this page?)

Your Perfectionist rating: _____

Measure the impact of your perfectionist.

What does your perfectionist say to you?

What impact does your perfectionist have on your life balance?

What would you like to say to your perfectionist?

The Procrastinator

Have you ever had an hour to get a bunch of stuff done, and then at fifty minutes, you find you haven't even started? Yeah, me too. Who doesn't love a great distraction? And with all the screens surrounding us at all times, it's easier than ever to fritter away the time. Every week there is a new, fabulous, time-wasting website just lying in wait for us to stumble upon it.

Time black holes include: social media (any flavor), email, online shopping, texting, talking on the phone (for those of us over 35), and video games. (Mobile is my poison, but it's not real gaming, according to my son. Phew.) And the list goes on.

Deep Thoughts about Brain Candy:

What is brain candy? Brain candy includes those activities which are fun and don't require a great deal of mental energy. Watching TV, surfing the internet, playing video games. Indulging in brain candy can be relaxing, even meditative.

My favorites include looking at real estate listings (when not looking to move), following celebrity gossip (who is that?), and, of course, Facebook (yes, I love your posts!). And because I know I'd be like a meth addict if I got into Pinterest or Houzz, I avoid those sites. (Yes, I am aware they are full of fantastic, even time-saving, ideas. Leave me alone.)

Is there anything wrong with brain candy? No. It can be a great way to unwind. But it takes time. And like real candy that wastes your calories, you need to acknowledge that you're making a time tradeoff when you indulge. (Sorry, hon, I can't read with you tonight because I was trying to beat that level on Candy Crush Saga – darn those last two jellies!)

If you need a break and want some brain candy – great. Just set a timer, say for twenty minutes, so you don't end up three hours into a marathon.

Productive Procrastination

Procrastination is sneaky. In addition to the obvious examples above, it can look (and be) productive. One example of productive procrastination is organizing your closet, sorting your sock drawer, or shopping for a wardrobe upgrade. Basically anything instead of finishing a laborious chore. At least something got done, right? Nevertheless, avoiding the most important task is still procrastination.

Perfectionist and Procrastinator

Procrastination and perfectionism can be a dangerous duo when they team up. Tinkering with presentation graphics or decorating your daughter's lunch bag is a double whammy of perfectionism that drives procrastination.

Page from My Playbook:

I LOVE books about clutter and home organization. So, as a world-class procrastinator, I've read every book about home organization and de-cluttering found in my county library system – probably more than thirty books.

When I admit this guilty pleasure, people often say, "Your house must be really organized!" Well, you'd think. But it's really all part of my strategy to procrastinate. (I also have read books about writing, to "prepare" me for writing. They contained some great tips, but at a certain point crossed the line to productive procrastination. It is a miracle this book got finished.)

Excuses, Excuses

Here are some of the excuses used by the procrastinator.

Pontifications by the procrastinator	Reality check
"I am just using this to relax."	Relaxation is a good goal, but if it comes at the expense of getting your responsibilities done, that is not helping your life balance.
"I am more efficient when I am under the gun. It makes me work better."	What would it feel like not to introduce voluntary stress into your life?
"I don't like to being so structured."	Fine. How's that working for you?
"I need to get psyched up before I can start."	Tick, tock. What's your process to get there?
[Insert your favorite excuse...]	What is that costing you?

Exercise: Rate your Procrastinator

How powerful is your procrastinator? Rate the following using a 1-5 scale.

1 = Not a problem.

5 = This is my middle name. (But, I'll worry about it tomorrow.)

Procrastinator rating: _____

Measure the impact of your procrastinator.

What are your favorite procrastination tools?

What are your "productive" procrastination tools?

What impact does your procrastinator have on your life balance?

The Hero

No story is complete without a hero, and playing the hero has definite payoffs. Being the go-to person feels good, and it's nice to be sought out or even just included. And it can often seem like the easiest thing to do. (*I'll just do it myself, that way I know it will get done correctly* – your perfectionist is helping out here as well.)

How do we play the hero at work? We might take on that additional assignment – even though we know we're already maxed out. Or we might say Yes when we're asked for help and then find ourselves taking over. Or our hero might always be found staying late, to "do whatever it takes." (And making sure everyone knows!)

At home, being a hero could mean not giving your family the opportunity to be productive and helpful. And if you are raising boys, you risk raising a lazy future husband. (Score points with your future daughter(s)-in-law, and let those sons step up!)

Once in a while, being the hero can be awesome. As a habit, it leaves something to be desired. For one thing, you train people to expect it. For another, playing the hero is not sustainable over time and can lead to resentment on your part or others'. And, let's face it—living martyrs are just plain annoying.

In addition to not being good for *you*, being a hero or over-functioning can also harm those around you. If you're the one continually taking all the opportunities, you block others from stepping up. Maybe they want or need the opportunity for personal or career growth.

Deep Thoughts about the Ball Hog:

Have you ever played a team sport, or watched your kids play, where one or more players is a total ball hog? Take basketball—this is the person who never passes and always takes the shot. They think they're doing a great job – racking up points for the team, but what about the rest of the players? Is that really a team effort? Sometimes, others want to take a shot, too. And that will build the entire team.

> **Page from My Playbook:**
>
> I was asked to give feedback on a presentation. The formatting was rough, so I just *had* to re-do it. This was a great procrastination opportunity for me because I rock at PowerPoint, and at the time I believed I was really being a hero.
>
> However, what I was really doing was over-functioning and likely insulting my colleague in the process. She had provided me a draft, not intended to be the final version. All she wanted was input on the key messages, for crying out loud!

Excuses, Excuses

Here are some common excuses we make to justify playing the hero.

Heroic hearsay	Reality check
"They need me. There is no one else."	Not true. It does not *always* have to be you.
"I've worked hard to work this hard."	Congratulations for living the dream.
"I'm not good at saying no."	You were not good at many things. With practice, you will get better.
"I love being helpful."	Great. What are you trading off?
[Insert your favorite excuse ....]	What is that costing you?

Exercise: Rate your Hero

How powerful is your Hero? Rate the following using a 1-5 scale.

1 = Not a problem.

5 = This is my middle name. (Not actually sure what anyone around me actually *does*, to justify their existence.)

Your Hero rating: _____

Measure the impact of your heroics.

What does your saboteur say to you that encourages your hero?

What do you get when you let your hero influence your decisions?

What would you like to say to your hero?

> **Deep Thoughts about Problems:**
>
> There are two kinds of problems in this world:
>
> > 1. My problem.
> > 2. Not my problem.
>
> Don't add things to bucket 1 that belong in bucket 2.

Now What?

So, you've spent some time figuring out your behavior traps. Now, let's look at ways to target your saboteur and break out of the Perfectionist, Procrastinator, and Hero habits.

Wrangle your Saboteur

You've put up with this unhelpful little voice long enough! Here are some tips for dealing with this threat to your life balance.

Stay on alert
The best defense against your saboteur is awareness. Just knowing that this voice is inserting itself into your daily life and decisions will help to drain its power.

When you're thinking negatively, ask yourself, "Is that me or my saboteur talking?"

Stage a power grab
If left unchecked, your saboteur can amass a great deal of power. You need to wrestle it back. Don't let her make decisions for you! When my saboteur mouths off, I tell her straight up, "It's none of your business." (Remember, fire that friend!)

Assign a role
If you feel like your saboteur sometimes has value to add, figure out how to use that to your advantage.

Define the role she gets to play. You choose. Can she be part of your advisory committee, to help you see potential pitfalls? Can the negative comments energize you to prove her wrong ("I'll show you!")?

Whatever the case, Decider and Approver are not roles she is allowed to play.

Flip the thoughts

If you're unable to avoid negative self-talk, try this. When you get a negative message, flip it, and state the opposite of that message. Then drop the first and hang onto the second.

Here's an example: "No one is going to buy your book, and if they do, they'll give you one star on Amazon and make a bunch of snarky comments." FLIP: "This book is going to be widely successful and provide tons of value to the readers, who will sing praises in their reviews and buy copies for all of their friends." Ahhh, much better.

Exercise: I Choose to...

One favorite weapon of the saboteur is to implant "I shoulds" into your life. Some of these are valid, but many are just noise. This is a simple but powerful exercise to help you gain control as you move from "I should" to "I choose."

Step 1:   Make a list of all the "I shoulds" in your head right now. It's likely a long list. The longer the better. This list can run the gauntlet from career to home, big things to small.

Build your entire list before moving to step 2.

Step 2:   Next, add a second column and change all of these statements to "I choose to..."

Page from My Playbook:

I did the "I choose" challenge. Here are some highlights from my list of over fifty.

I should	I choose to
Work more.	Work more efficiently.
Waste less time at work by not chatting with people.	Continue to build connections, but make them shorter and schedule them to be less interruption-driven.
Stop promising things I will not do.	Stop promising things I will not do.
Prepare healthier meals at home.	Keep it as healthy as possible; okay to be simple and convenient. Dinner is about family, not just food.
See if I can return my mattress.	Let it go. Stop. Thinking. About. It.

Roll up your sleeves and get to work. Make this list as long as possible. Remember, do all of "I should" the go back to "I choose to".

I should (page 1)	I choose to

I should (continued)	I choose to

Exercise: Tell Her Off!

Write a Dear Jane letter or email to break up with your saboteur, telling her that she is no longer welcome to share her opinions or ideas with you. Feel free to use strong language (like "go jump in a lake" or some such). If you prefer – feel free to make a video.

Note: If your saboteur is a big issue for you, you might want explore one of the many great books on this topic. Search on "inner critic," "gremlin," or "inner voice" for options.

Rehabilitate your Perfectionist

If you have found perfectionist tendencies to be one of your opportunity areas, consider these tips to combat your perfectionist.

Give yourself permission

Like the unattainable beauty of airbrushed super models, doing everything you'd like to do perfectly is just not compatible with good life balance.

So, give yourself permission not to be perfect at everything. Whether it's having a less than spotless and organized house, missing an occasional soccer game, or skipping a meeting not critical to your success or vice versa. It's okay. The universe will adjust, I promise.

Move the bar . . . down

Many times, we set our own bar of what is acceptable. We can be influenced by cultural norms and peer pressure to set a certain level of perfectionism in life. Here are two points on one spectrum:

- Option A: Kids in freshly pressed clothes carrying a lunch of sushi and homemade kale chips with a daily hand-written note of encouragement. Homework complete and has been copied to eliminate any eraser marks. Kids arrive to school fifteen minutes early to let them have a leisurely walk to class.
- Option B: Kids in reasonably clean clothes (you think), homework complete (you're pretty sure) and lunch money in their account (you hope). Beat the bell! Boo-ya!

Decide what works for you and your family and call that success. ("Family" here is defined exclusively as the people who live in your house. Not mothers-in-law, best friends, sisters, or well-meaning grandmothers.)

Page from My Playbook:

When we were planning our wedding, I decided that I did not want the perfect wedding. (My husband-to-be did not utter strong opinions in this area. One more indication that I was marrying a smart guy.) What I wanted was a really *fun* wedding and reception.

To help ensure this, I declared a set of very specific and achievable success criteria. 1. Groom shows up. 2. Pastor shows up. 3. No one gets food poisoning. That was it.

So when they played the wrong music as I walked down the aisle, when I spilled on my dress, when my hair tumbled out of its "up-do," requiring some creative cover up – I didn't care. Everyone was having fun, not the least of which were my brand-new husband and me! (Especially after I swapped my torture shoes for sport sandals.)

Redefine "done"

Do you struggle to get things done? Yeah, me too. It's time to redefine DONE. What does that really mean anyway? Remember the 80/20 rule. Sometimes enough is enough!

Page from My Playbook:

I had worked for months putting together a global strategic plan. I had done primary and secondary research, interviews, data analysis, you name it. It was all coming together in the plan that would lead my company into the future. (Forgive the hyperbole. It was a lot of work. I like to think it mattered, at least a little.) At the end, I got paralyzed by what I might be forgetting, what could make it better.

I was lamenting with a colleague, and he gave me the brilliant advice, "Sometimes, you just have to push print." Call it done, call it complete, and move on.

> And guess what – I did and it was. (And I am working to apply this principle for this book as well!)

Bust through analysis paralysis

Here is a process for dealing with analysis paralysis when it arrives:

1. List your top two or three choices (no more).
2. Evaluate and select.
3. Move on. Don't rehash the decision.

Why only 2-3 choices? If there are more than that number still truly in the running, you don't know what you want. Hmmm, maybe you could even skip it entirely.

How much time should you spend? Larger decisions obviously invite more analysis. Use a scale to help you gauge the right investment. Here are some rules that work for me. Under $100 - no more than 10 minutes. Under $500 – under 30 minutes. Above $500 – will vary, depending on whether I can buy it at Costco and let their buyers do the filtering for me.

Set the rules that work for you and release yourself from the need for "full" information.

Page from My Playbook:

My son has tens of thousands of Legos. They had taken over his room and were threatening to spill out into the rest of the house. (If you have ever stepped on a Lego with bare feet, you can appreciate the importance of needing to contain them.) They were in random bins, on the floor and on every horizontal surface. It was time to get a system. So I went to the Promised Land of organization, the Container Store. And because time is short in my life too, it was part of date night.

After a reasonable amount of time, my husband, who does not share my fanatical attraction to potentially life-changing storage systems, found me in one of the aisles looking for the perfect solution. He counseled me, "Don't let the perfect be the enemy of the good." (Paraphrasing Voltaire as it turns out – who knew?) That perspective took the pressure off and allowed me to quit worrying and just decide. And it got us on to our date night before the restaurants closed.

The plastic drawers are now the cornerstone of the Lego storage system. (They also provided an awesome procrastination opportunity for me, via the sorting exercise, but that's another story.)

Exercise: Perfect No More

List five things that you are going to lower the bar on.

Looking at your list above, who set the bar on these in the first place?

What else can you do to combat perfectionism?

Re-train the Procrastinator

I've listed below some changes you can make to help with your procrastination challenges. Do it now. Don't put it off for later. I am on to you!

Schedule it

When you have an important appointment or meeting, you put in on your calendar. Time Management 101. Use your calendar to block time when you have a project or an activity you want to do as well.

The act of writing it down or entering it online will do several things: it increases your accountability, demonstrates its importance, and actually allocates time to do it. Activities, projects, workouts—anything that is relegated to "when you have time"—just won't get done in a busy life.

Create intermediate deadlines

Procrastination can be even more of a challenge when a project is big and overwhelming. I get it. I am writing a book with no deadline. But knowing what you need or can do next can be a huge help in accomplishing any project. Take these steps to assist you.

1. Identify the next possible step that has no prior dependencies.
2. Develop a SMART goal for that step.

If you've never heard this tried-and-true workplace term before, SMART goals are specific, measureable, attainable, relevant, and time-bound. They help you be clear on what you need to do.

Instead of saying "I am going to organize my digital pictures." Say, "by next Friday, I will organize five years of digital pictures." Or you can get even more specific: "Thursday, between 8-10 pm, I am going to locate all my picture files from 2011, put them in the same place, and sort them into categories: 1. Best of (with subcategory, I-look-amazing-and-must-print-immediately); 2. Videos; 3. Ignore and just maybe delete someday. And because I am super responsible, I will create a back-up while I am at it."

Make sure to block time on your calendar to do it, include the deadline, and be specific about what you'd like to accomplish.

Trick yourself

Often the first step is the hardest. Here's a tip I've heard relating to exercise as well as home organization. Set a timer and tell yourself you just have to do the activity for, let's say, twenty minutes. The time limit makes it much easier to commit to getting started, because, come on – you can do twenty minutes!

When the time is up, oftentimes, you just use the momentum to keep going. And if not, you still got twenty minutes' worth done!

Heidi's Story:

Heidi was training for a marathon (I know, crazy, right?). At one point in her training, she was burned out and really, really did not want to do her training run. How did she get through it? Small wins.

1. Get dressed for running. (Yea, me!)
2. Drive to training run. (I'm here.)
3. Run for 10 minutes. (I can do it my sleep.)
4. Keep going. (Might as well....)

Make re-engaging easy

Leave something easy to pick up like a final proofread or typing in edits. If you know you will have a quick win, it will help motivate you to get started. And the small victory will be motivating to tackle the next step in the project. (Caution: make sure to move on to the tough stuff, and don't just fill your time doing the simple stuff.)

Celebrate victories

So many life tasks are a never ending merry-go-round: laundry, cooking, status reports, homework, housework, you name it. And there is no gold star for keeping up.

So create that gold star for yourself. Notice and appreciate small victories. Don't wait for a promotion or six-page spread in *Architectural Digest* to celebrate where you are.

When your house is clean (enough), take a deep breath and smile. Laundry done? Cheers to you! Work assignment completed? Another job well done! Everyone fed and in bed? You have provided one more day of necessary nourishment to your family. Congratulations!

Kory's Story:

Kory is an amazing kindergarten teacher with a husband and two sporty girls. She's also the ranger responsible for Mount Laundry that sometimes appears in their house after a particularly busy time. When she summits Mount Laundry (gets it all washed and distributed), she celebrates her conquest by declaring a happy dance and issuing a self-congratulations on Facebook. (Next time you see a post like that – make sure and congratulate your friend! Well done!)

Exercise: Let's Celebrate!

Make a list of at least five (big or small) accomplishments that you can remind yourself to celebrate?

What type of celebration would you like?

What other procrastination breakers will you try?

Redeploy the Hero

If your inner hero is carrying the weight of the world and collapsing underneath it, here are some retraining tips.

Don't assume your way is best

There's more than one way to swing a stuffed cat (how's that for political correctness?). And there's also more than one way to run a meeting. Create a presentation. Load a dishwasher. Fold a towel. Get your kids ready for school. [Insert your favorite here.] Unless you are having a teaching moment – let people do things their way.

Encourage and celebrate others' successes

It's easy to fall into the comparison trap. This can be keeping up with the Joneses on the car you drive, trying to emulate others in your workplace, or making sure your kids' lunches look like they were made by Martha Stewart.

Stop it. Right now.

You need to solve for you. Remember, no one else walks in your shoes. Make your life work for you. Let others design lives that work for them and celebrate with them.

Let others volunteer first

If you often jump and volunteer for projects, you have trained others to expect that you'll do so. Practice not being the first person to respond. Try to allow at least two others to respond before you do.

Get off the critical path

At work, are you the go-to gal or guy? Do people like to pull you in because you're awesome? If you answered Yes to either of those questions, does that still mean you need to be part of everything? No. Say it with me now: No. I do not need to be part of everything.

Embrace the old Polish proverb – "Not my circus, not my monkey."

Work for impact – not activity

Keep yourself focused on what will make the biggest difference, not what will make you look the busiest.

Exercise: Drop the Cape

Think of five areas where you might be playing the hero. Decide if you will complete it, shut it down or hand it off.

How will you keep from being sucked in again?

Exercise: Extreme Change

To help you get creative with how you can tackle your culprits, make a list of the most extreme scenarios you can think of. Treat this exercise like a brainstorming session with no bad ideas. You can even do this with a friend (over wine, perhaps). Once you have your crazy list – think of what you could really apply.

Example: Extreme Change

Extreme changes you can make to help your life balance.

First draft of anything is the only and final draft.
Never clean my house again.
No more than three minutes for any decision.
Say no to everything that is asked of me.

Now it's your turn. Have fun with this.

Extreme changes you can make to help your life balance.

For each of the above, what it a scaled back version you could try?

Now let's take a look at the role of others in our lives.

DETERMINE the Role of Others

My introvert husband has been known to say, "My life would be perfect, if it weren't for all those other people." As an extrovert, I look at him like he has three heads, but sometimes I recognize he has a point (just don't tell him I said that!). Setting priorities for yourself *is* much easier when you are just planning for . . . . well . . . yourself.

But most of us have other important people in our lives. People who matter to us and influence the choices we make. These people will impact your life, but remember, they are not you. In your life, *you* are the star and director. You get to choose the role others play. And given our interconnected lives, we need to learn how to manage these relationships to work for us.

This chapter's mindset:

- Be honest about how people are impacting you.
- Don't worry about being rude.
- Be selfish and name what you really want.

By the end of this chapter you will have

1. Identified your VIPs.
2. Described how they influence your life.
3. Found some retraining opportunities.

> **Deep Thoughts about Flight Attendants:**
>
> On every flight, you've seen and heard the flight attendants show you how to put on the yellow masks that will come down from the ceiling, in the unlikely event of a sudden loss of cabin pressure. They tell you to put your own mask on before helping others, which, if you're flying with your kids, goes against millions of years of ingrained parental instincts.
>
> Did you ever wonder what the airlines have against kids? It turns out, nothing. Without the mask, you would pass out very quickly. And if you fell unconscious, what use would you be to anyone?
>
> Apply this concept to your life. Take care of yourself first.

Your Inner Circle

Life balance is not created (or ruined) in isolation. To help with your life-balance journey, the next step is to take a closer look at the other people in your life. Unless you plan to live in solitude in a fortified compound somewhere, you'll need to figure out the players in your life.

Exercise: VIP ID

For this exercise, make of list of the key people in your life.

Step 1:   Make a list of people in your life who currently influence the choices you make (whether they know it or not). This could be a long list.

Step 2:   After you complete your list, review it and circle the top 5-6 whom you *choose* to allow to influence your life.

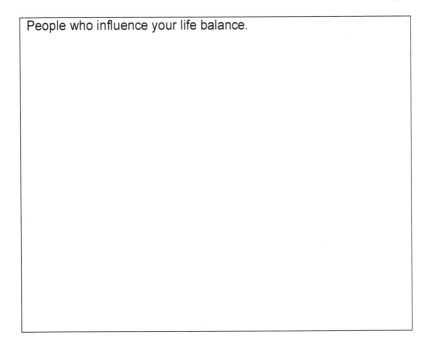

People who influence your life balance.

The circled names are your VIPs (Very Important Persons).

Exercise: VIP Influence

Next, you're looking for people who negatively impact your life balance more than you'd like.

Step 1: In the next chart, list any of your VIPs who have *too much influence* on your life balance.

Step 2: Get specific about the areas where they have too much influence.

These VIPs are not intentionally trying to ruin your life. This is not a blaming exercise, rather we are looking for causes and opportunities.

Here are some fictional examples for you. As you can see, this information can be sensitive. Consider how you will keep it private so you can be completely honest here.

Who?	Things they do that impact your life balance
Spouse	Doesn't do enough around the house.
Kids	Too many sports games/practices – too much driving.
Manager	Last-minute meetings at 5pm. Fire drills caused by poor planning. False emergencies caused by ego.
Co-workers	Waste too much of my time by socializing. Don't always meet commitments.
Friend(s)	Opposite - wish I had more time with friends.
Family	Too many extended family activities. Bi-weekly dinners are too much.

Now you try.

Who?	Things they do that impact your life balance

Take Back Control

As you think about your VIP list and their influence areas, ask yourself these questions:

- What do you give them, time-wise?
- Is it more than they expect?
- More than they need?
- Has this always been the case?

With that food for thought, here are some tips to help re-calibrate your relationships with your VIPs.

Get explicit

In relationships, it's easy to fall in to patterns that we didn't choose. They just happen. These could be division of labor, expectations on response times, or what you're willing to do to complete a work assignment, just to name a few examples. And these unspoken expectations can have a negative impact on life balance.

If you have "agreements" like this in your life that are bothering you, spell them out. If you don't like where they land – re-negotiate.

Manage expectations

Can't make a deadline? Need to opt out of the next big volunteer opportunity? The key is to make sure people are not expecting you. Raise the white flag and inform those who need to know what you can and cannot do. And do this as early as possible, to give people notice so they can plan.

Re-contract

If you will be making dramatic behavior changes, you may need to re-contract overtly with people. This involves acknowledging the status quo, clearly laying out recommended changes, and seeking agreement and commitment to those changes.

Think of a building contractor. When you make a change to your plans (e.g., now I really want you to move the door as well), you negotiate the changes and update the contract appropriately. You may not do this in writing, but the agreement definitely changes.

Let 'em wait

Whether it is answering every email within minutes of receiving it or jumping up to see what your kids are calling out for now, avoid having a Pavlovian response to interruption stimuli. Let the interrupters wait and engage on your terms.

It's still about you

Take a minute to think about your own behaviors. How might they be contributing to others' impact on your life balance? Does your Hero show up? How about your Perfectionist? Would your Procrastinator (secretly) rather drive carpool than finish that work project? Does your saboteur convince you that you need to do it all?

Cathy's Story:

Cathy was working on a fast-growing team with a start-up culture. Her role was to help manage the finances, monitor sales, and serve as a strategic resource for the VP. However, she found administrative tasks kept ending up on her to-do list. She knew that the entire team was very busy and that the real admin was also overloaded, so being a good team player, she wanted to help.

These tasks began to distract from her real role, however, until it was no longer a matter of "helping out." To help reset, she proactively went through her to-do list and identified those things she would no longer do. She then went to her team and unapologetically (this is key!) said, "You will have to find a new way to get X done."

When requests continued to come in, she said, "No, I am not able to do that for you." Although it seemed a bit intimidating at first, by having these conversations in a professional manner, she was able to reset expectations and focus on delivering on her most important projects.

Exercise: VIP Privileges

To get the most value from this step, it's critical that you be honest with yourself. NO guilt trips allowed! Clearly understanding and making tradeoffs to improve your life balance will mean that (gasp!) sometimes you will choose yourself over others. Take a deep breath. It will be okay.

Step 1: Go back to your VIP Influence list and copy the top ones in the next table.

Step 2: For each, ask yourself what role you played in creating the specific dynamic.

Step 3: Now determine what you can change in your behavior to make the situation better. Be specific.

Step 4: Also, name one thing (minimum) that you can ask your VIP for to make it better. Again, be as specific as possible.

Here is an example to get you started.

Who?	Things they do/don't do that impact your life balance	What can you do differently?	What can you ask others to do/not do?
Spouse	Doesn't do enough around the house.	Don't jump in and do it. Don't criticize when they do help.	Help with specific chores
Kids	Too many sports games – too much driving.	Skip some games.	Look for carpool opportunities. Limit activities.
Manager	Last-minute meetings at 5pm. False emergencies caused by poor planning or ego.	Clarify asks. Decline meeting requests.	No 5pm meetings. More notice on assignments.
Co-workers	Waste too much of my time by socializing. Don't deliver on time.	Say when you are busy/on deadline.	Limit interruptions and schedule lunch or coffee break.

Now, it's your turn again.

Who?	Things they do/don't do that impact your life balance	What can you do differently?	What can you ask others to do/not do?

Take Action!

Optimizing your relationships to support your life balance will only happen if you actually make changes. Make a commitment, schedule it and do it!

List three things you will do differently. Give yourself a deadline.

List three things you will ask others for. Give yourself a deadline. (And really do it!)

If this makes you uncomfortable, that's okay. Do it anyway.

Now that we have looked at your relationships, let's take a look at decision-making.

DECIDE Smarter

How many decisions do you make every day? I'm sure some PhD candidate somewhere has come up with a conclusive (or at least defensible) answer to this question, but for our purposes, let's just say...a lot. Take your best guess, quadruple it and use that number.

Of all these decisions, I would venture that most of them you probably don't even notice.

One of the ways to improve your life balance is to recognize when you are making decisions that will impact it and being thoughtful and intentional about the choices you make.

This chapter digs into decision-making and trains you to make better daily decisions that will improve your life balance.

We're going to keep a few of last chapter's mindsets for this one as well:

- Be selfish. Decide what is best for you. Yes, you.
- Be fearless and practice solving for yourself.

By the end of this chapter you will have

- Learned to recognize and make better tradeoffs.
- Accepted responsibility for your tradeoffs.
- Embraced the power of No.
- Strengthened your Yes.

Your Responsibility

Here's an idea. If you're unhappy with results of the choices you're making, make different ones! This is rather flippant, and I know this is not easy, but bear with me.

I believe that most of us have more control over our lives than we take responsibility for. We need to embrace that control in order to optimize our life balance.

As the risk of stating the obvious, when you make decisions, don't continue to make choices that don't work for you, that don't bring you closer to your designed life. Make decisions and tradeoffs that *do* work for you and help you build the life you want.

Keep reading to get some tools and skills to help you.

Decisions, Decisions

When it comes to life balance, there are three types of decisions that have a huge impact.

- Making tradeoffs and choosing between options.
- Deciding what gets added to your life.
- Deciding what gets removed from your life.

> **Deep Thoughts about Big Rocks:**
>
> Have you heard of the big rocks experiment? You know, there's a large jar and three piles of rocks beside it which you need to put into the jar. Big rocks, medium rocks and small pebbles. Spoiler alert: if you start with the pebbles, all the rocks won't fit. The secret is to put the big rocks in first. You then put in the medium rocks and finally the pebbles.
>
> The problem with this "solution" is that, even though you've squeezed them all in, can you actually lift the jar? They never show that part! Is there any breathing room left?
>
> How about this for an alternate strategy? Sort the pebbles and only keep those that are most valuable to you. Leave the others out of the jar. Or even leave out some of the medium or big rocks. Scandalous! But *voilà* – a lighter jar and a little breathing room!

It's a Trick! Yes = No

Think of those three-word sentences which have had a huge impact on your life. I love you. I am sorry. Can we add one more to that list? How about "Yes or no"? This phrase, often implied rather than spoken, is one of the most common ones you encounter.

But instead of "Yes or No," you need to relearn this one as "Yes = No." That's right, Yes = No.

When you say Yes to something, you are implicitly saying No to something else. I repeat, when you say Yes to something, you are saying No to something else. Think about that, and let it settle for a moment. (Please embrace the truth of this statement versus searching your mind for exceptions. Thank you.)

Tradeoff Training

To illustrate Yes = No, think about every decision as a tradeoff. Choosing X over Y.

Although we do this all day long, we usually don't notice when we are making a tradeoff.

In order to live something closer to the life you want and improve your life balance, *these invisible tradeoffs must become thoughtful and deliberate.* Being intentional with these tradeoffs will allow you to regain control of your life. No one can do everything. The key is deciding on what you want most and optimizing for that.

Remember the silver bullet?

> Decide what you want, and build your life to make it true.
> Make decisions and tradeoffs that best honor your life priorities.

Make each choice in service to the life you want. The one you have designed. Stay off autopilot. Do not let others decide for you. This simple step will increase control of your life and improve your life balance.

Name the Tradeoffs

Let's look at some typical decisions that may come your way.

- Will I work late tonight?
- Will I check my email this weekend?
- Will I go for that job with lots of travel?
- Will I have a date night with my spouse?
- Will I exercise tonight?
- Will I answer just one more email tonight?
- Will I let Meggie sign up for softball *and* soccer?

What if you looked at the same questions as tradeoff opportunities?

- Will I work late *or* get home for dinner with my family?
- Will I check my email *or* completely unplug and refresh this weekend?
- Will I go for that job with lots of travel *or* choose a role that will keep me local?
- Will I have a date night with my spouse *or* stay in with the kids?
- Will I exercise tonight *or* read a book to my child?

- Will I answer that one more email tonight *or* go to bed without work being foremost in my mind?
- Will I let Meggie sign up for softball and soccer *or* help her prioritize, to allow dinner at home a few nights a week?

As you can see, each decision is actually a tradeoff. To choose one thing is to give up another.

Some of the scenarios listed above are pretty simple, and I realize that many of your tradeoffs are not so straightforward. And sometimes you may have only unattractive choices, which lead to really tough tradeoffs.

However, recognizing that you are making a tradeoff and being clear about what you are choosing between will help you have better life balance. You may not like the choice you make, but you'll know why you made the tradeoff you did. There is power in choice.

Increase Intentionality

The following are steps to take when you're making a tradeoff so you can thoughtfully choose the right option for you. This might seem cumbersome, but it's really fast in real life.

1   Identify when you're making a tradeoff (hint, always).
2   Clearly outline the top options.
3   Decide which option best supports your life priorities and success criteria.
4   Weigh in the needs of your VIPs (if appropriate).
5   Determine the best tradeoff.

If you are stuck – try this. Say these statements out loud.

- I am choosing to _____.
- This means I will not be able to _____.
- The benefit of this choice is _____.
- The cost of this choice is _____.
- This is the right tradeoff because _____.

If the decision is uncomfortable, ask yourself the following questions:

- Who are you serving best with this decision?
- Is it worth it?

Exercise: Tradeoff Practice

List five recent tradeoffs you have had to make. Write them as a choice.

Here are a few examples.

Will I... [Choice 1]	Or will I... [Choice 2]
Work late tonight.	Go for a run.
Sign up for a class.	Spend more time at home.
Stay up and finish my book.	Sleep and feel refreshed tomorrow.

Your turn again.

Will I... [Choice 1]	Or will I... [Choice 2]

Circle the choice you made.

> What does articulating choices and deciding do for you?

In addition to trade-offs, sometimes, you will have explicit requests that come your way. They can very clearly be seen as a Yes/No question. Next, let's take a look at the two sides of the Yes/No coin.

The Gatekeeper

Like a mama bear with her cubs behind her in the cave, be the gatekeeper to your life of balance. Protect it from unwanted intruders. (But try not to hurt anyone.)

When you get a request for something, be the gatekeeper. Remember, the good news is that yes/no questions do have two possible answers. Yes, which is often the default, and No. Otherwise the question is rhetorical. (Kids know and love this loophole. "Can you take out the trash?" "No." "Let me rephrase that. Take out the trash.")

In fact, No is one of the first power words we learn as children. If you have recently been around a verbal toddler, you will have hear them use this word boldly, unabashedly and often. Such power. However, as we get older and improve our manners, we stop leaning on this power word to shape and control our lives. Well, it's time to rejuvenate the No in your life.

No 101
How to say no.

- With a smile. Requests are not assignments.
- Say it clearly. People hear what they want to hear. Don't risk a "Maybe" being translated into a "Yes."

- Give your answer as soon as possible, so people can move on to plan B.
- Only say, "I'll think about it" if you truly are thinking about it.
- Lose the guilt!

Deep thoughts about Discomfort:

"But it's so hard to say no!" you protest. "I feel guilty when I do."

Remember, one minute of discomfort is better than a long-term commitment you resent.

Social Nos and No-Nos

Even social engagements have an impact on life balance that is not always positive. Here are some tips on saying no in your social life.

- Don't say Yes and then not show up. This is rude.
- Don't say Yes and cancel at the last minute. If it's not a true emergency, this is also rude.
- It is okay to say No. Even if you don't have other plans.
- Know that you may quit getting asked. This is not rude.

No at work

At work, actually saying No directly can feel too strong. It may pay to be more nuanced. Here are some tips to help ensure new projects aren't landing on your plate every day.

- Make sure you are clear on the request.
- Understand the goal of the request. Perhaps there is another way to meet their goal.
- Ask for help making tradeoffs with other work commitments.
- Make sure the requestor understands the scope of what (you think) they are asking. Feel free to educate them. (This project will take about ten hours to do. Is that investment worth it?)
- Make sure they are not just thinking out loud. "Wouldn't it be great if..." does not always need to turn into an assignment.
- Put it in terms that they care about. (Note: this often does not include your life balance.)

> **Deep thoughts about Responsibility:**
>
> Life balance is a personal responsibility. Full stop. Your workplace may or may not claim to care about your life balance. And even if they do, no one else can make your life balance happen.
>
> Ask for what you need, but keep it professional and on their terms. You have limits to what you can do and workplaces need to accept that. Workplaces have needs, and you also need to respect that. You need to draw the line where it works for both parties. Cathy did a great job of this in her story in the Decide section.

The Savvy Yes

Saying yes is more fun than saying no (even your mouth looks happier with a Yes), and it can easily become our default. However, by defaulting to Yes (or "Sure," if you are from the Midwest), you give away your control. Here are some ways to make your Yes a thoughtful one:

Ask for clarity

Before agreeing to anything, you should have a clear understanding of what you are signing up for. Although this sounds obvious, this is a critical step in not overcommitting. And when people say, "Don't worry, it's not that much work," you should "trust, but verify," to quote Ronald Reagan. Get the details before you commit, not after. Do not make assumptions.

The more clarity you have, not only will you know better whether to say yes, it will also make it easier to accomplish the task when you start. Better still, clarity will ensure the person who is asking will get what they're asking for. Win-win-win.

Take time to decide

If they need an answer right away, do not let their deadline force you into a bad decision. Take a Time-Out.. Before any Yes, take a few seconds at a minimum to really think about the implications and the tradeoffs required to honor that Yes. And if it will take a day or two to make the right tradeoff – by all means, don't commit on the spot.

Ask yourself:

- What will I need to say no to, in order to do this?
- Does this support my priorities?
- If not, who am I doing this for? Is that okay?
- Will the impact on my life balance be worth it?

Make a counteroffer

You don't always have to say yes or no. Try a counteroffer. "Here's what I can do." This also lets you clarify what is needed and sets expectations. If your counteroffer is not of interest...then No, it is.

Kim's Story:

Kim was asked to be the chairperson for the school walk-a-thon fundraiser. This was an all-day event needing about eighty volunteers in shifts, snacks, logistics, and many other moving pieces.

Kim loved this event and wanted to assist, but she knew the chair role would take more time than she could commit. From participating in the past, she knew that the volunteer coordinator was a critical role, so she said no to the chair role and counteroffered to take on the role of volunteer coordinator.

Buyer's Remorse

If you say yes to something and immediately know it was a mistake, reverse yourself then and there. If you wait too long, it will be more difficult to get out of the commitment and much less respectful of the other person. The goal is to take care of yourself, not to put others in a bind by being unreliable. Admit your mistake, decide what's possible and communicate clearly.

Page from My Playbook:

When my youngest started kindergarten and my oldest was in 2nd grade, I trooped up to the school and signed up to work in their classes each week. However, that night I felt overwhelmed by this commitment (one that, yes, I volunteered for).

I immediately emailed both teachers and explained that I had overcommitted and would not be a weekly volunteer in their classroom. This allowed them to plan accordingly and me to take back some time and forego any resentfulness I might have harbored. Boy, did that feel great!

Exercise: Why, Why, Why Did I Say Yes?

Think about a time when you said yes, but wish you had said no. What could you have done differently? Replay the scene in your mind. This time, create a new response using one or more of the suggestions above.

Now that you've learned about deciding what lives on your to-do list, let's dig into other ways to improve your life balance.

DO What it Takes

It's time to get practical and tactical. This chapter is filled with specific tips to increase your efficiency and improve your use of technology to support your life balance.

Your mindset for this chapter:
- Be open to new ideas.
- Be willing to try a few of them.

By the end of this chapter, you will have

1. Learned efficiency tips.
2. Defined your micro-culture.

The efficiency-improving actions will complement your smart tradeoffs by helping you get more done in less time.

Unitask

Research is coming out daily on the fallacy of multi-tasking. You aren't really multi-tasking – you're just doing two things, alternating very quickly between them. And you lose a ton of efficiency this way. Really. There are studies about this. It's not just the internet saying so.

If you are unfamiliar with the concept, let me define unitasking.

1. Do *one* thing at a time.
2. Get it done or to a natural stopping point.
3. Stop.

Unitasking can be hard to do and will take practice if it's new. However, you will be amazed at how productive you can be when you're only trying to do one thing. You actually get things done!

Another element to unitasking is to be *fully present* in whatever you are doing. Give whatever you're doing 100% attention, whether it be work, time with your kids, volunteer time, or however you are spending your time. People notice when you're only half there, and it isn't as satisfying for you either. (And put down that phone!)

Limit Interruptions

Once you have buckled down to do some work, do everything in your power to limit interruptions. Interruptions are just invitations to stop your work and do work for someone else. Or just to goof off.

- **Turn off notifications.** These are the not-helpful interruptions (**DING**) your email program provides every time a new email arrives. Turn them all the way off. Do not set to vibrate. Do this for your PC and your phone.
- **Instant messages.** It is okay to ignore instant messages when they come in. If you know you won't be able to resist, block messages during your work time.
- **Texting.** If you are a frequent texter – turn off notifications for them as well. (If your nanny texts ONLY to announce trips to the ER, however, there's some wiggle room here.)

- **Phone calls.** Same rules apply. Turn off the ringer and let it go to voicemail.
- **Train others.** Warn your VIPs about your interruption blockers, to help set expectations. But be careful about teaching them the workarounds.

Use Email Wisely

Email. Friend or foe? Here are some ways to get the most out of your email while letting it take less out of you.

- **Send less.** The less you send, the less you receive. Be thoughtful about what you communicate in email and to whom. Copy only who is necessary.
- **Do not Reply All.** Don't be part of the problem. Please.
- **Slow your response time.** Sit on emails a minimum of one hour. Four hours is better. Do this as part of your retraining.
- **Limit email checks.** Ideally to 1-2 times per day. Put it on your calendar. Do not check email other times of the day. If needed, put on an out-of-office message declaring this intention.
- **Close email.** During your dedicated work time, shut the program entirely. You wouldn't answer if you were in a meeting (or you shouldn't); treat your heads-down work time with as much respect.
- **Don't use your inbox as to-do list.** Use the tasks function for your to-do list. (I resisted this for years. It really works!)
- **Use folders.** As you soon as you have read an email, deal with it, delete it or file it.
- **Be clear and concise.** Help others by getting to your point quickly and if there is a request, call it out clearly.
- **Talk instead.** Real time, voice-activated interaction IRL (in real life). Revolutionary.

Be the Boss of your Calendar

Here are a few tips to make your calendar work harder for you.

- **Quitting time.** Do you plan to leave the office at 5:00pm? Block your calendar at 5:00 to signal you are not available. Treat it like a meeting and leave on time.

- **Personal time.** Need to leave at 3:30 to drive carpool? Mark yourself as not available (even out of office) to make sure you don't get double-booked. Back online and working at 4:00? – keep it open for that time. Be honest about it. Subterfuge induces stress.
- **Work time.** Block time in your day when you are most productive to do your own work. (Also known as your day job.) Protect it from meetings. And don't waste prime time on email. You are not being selfish, you are being smart.
- **Honor appointments with yourself.** Treat them like any other important meeting. Move them if you need to, but make sure you reschedule them immediately, don't just delete.
- **Deadlines.** Put your intermediate deadlines on your calendar to increase your chances of delivering on time.
- **Be realistic.** If you're always late, you're not building in enough time to do things, get places, whatever. Either get better at estimating the time needed or cut yourself off when the time is done.
- **Don't double-book yourself.** You're only one person and can only be one place at a time. (See "Unitasking" above.)

Corral Your Meetings

In many work places, meetings can take over your entire day if you let them. Protect your time and yourself from useless meetings. If you need to be there (and always question if you do), do your part to optimize the time spent.

- **Insist on an agenda.** Ideally sent in advance, but at a minimum, clearly stated at the beginning of the meeting. Everyone should be clear on "What do we need to accomplish in the next 55 minutes? What decisions need to be made?"
- **Be on time.** Being late is not a charming personality trait. No one cares that you are busy. They are too.
- **Ask targeted questions.** If things are stalling or going off topic, bring back the original goals with a thoughtful question.
- **Be a time-keeper.** Remind people not only of the time, but also of the progress toward the goal. "We have five minutes left to close on these issues."

- **Ask for decisions.** This can be a question: "What is the decision?" Or it may be a re-articulation of what you believe the decision is on the table. "I believe we are agreeing to XYZ. Is that correct?"
- **End at least five minutes early.** This will allow you to get to your next meeting on time as well as have a small little breather in between. (We drink a lot of coffee in Seattle.)
- **Skip some.** Do you add and receive value at every meeting you are in? If not, don't go. Be courteous and decline the meeting, tentative responses are useless for organizers.

Create a Micro-Culture

Organizations often talk about the company culture and team culture. I challenge you to create your own micro-culture. Another way to say this is to march to your own drumbeat. Do what works for you. Solve for you. Here are some starter tips for a healthy micro-culture.

- **Quit the face-time game.** Some career advisors will tell you to be the first in the office and last to leave. Playing the face-time game is competing in the wrong event. Even if you win, you lose.
- **Focus on results, not activity.** Time does not equal output. Time does not equal results. At the end of the day, work toward results (SMART goals again). Don't just be busy. It's easy to be busy.
- **Be proactive.** Some jobs are by their nature very reactive, which can be difficult to predict. If possible, try to organize your work life to be primarily proactive. If you control the rhythm and the timing, it's more likely to work for you.
- **Plan ahead.** If you have seasonality (busy and less busy times), use this knowledge to your advantage. If you know that your busy time is coming up, limit other commitments.

Exercise: Your Micro-Culture

Write a description of your aspirational micro-culture as if you are answering the question, "What is it like to work there?" Be bold here. What do you want to it be?

Page from My Playbook:

Here's my micro-culture. I work in a results-oriented, flexible team. I am able to get my work done through a combination of modified traditional office hours and remote work. I am very clear in my commitments and honor them highly and expect that of others. I value efficiency and limit unnecessary emails and meetings. I engage in non-work connection time with my teammates to build relationships and serve my extrovert social needs.

Finding the right role: I also knew I wanted a mostly proactive role. At one point, I was offered a very cool role that would have had a great deal of customer interaction, which I loved. However, the role would also be unpredictable as much of the customer interaction would be urgent. Therefore, I knew accepting the role would introduce a ton of extra stress in my life. Instead, I moved in the direction of working on longer-term projects. These were still challenging and interesting, but I was able to have more control over the schedule and not have to be in pure reactive mode all the time.

Now you.

Describe the micro-culture you want to work in.

If your micro-culture cannot coexist with your team or organization culture, you will need to choose which will take precedence. Do you choose to embrace and embody the macro-culture? Or will you choose what works for you?

Prioritize and Delete Stuff

This cleanse won't make you drink only juice for a week, but it will make you carefully look at what is on your plate to see what can come off. This list also contains hints on how to keep things from getting added to your to-do list.

- **Take a reality check.** Ask yourself, "What's the worst that happens if I don't do this?" "What's the best that happens?" "Can anyone else do this just as well, or help me do this?"
- **Remove activities.** If they don't support your priorities, or just make you too busy, jettison them (at least for now). Remember that most kids' activities come with round-trip transportation needs provided by....
- **Purposefully procrastinate.** A smart delay can make the need go away. Think you need to run out/go online and buy something? Put it off for a week (or even a day). If you've stopped thinking about it, skip it.
- **Prioritize what is visible.** Really in a pinch? Pick the things that people will notice and which matter most and skip the rest.
- **Be less nosy.** Hero alert! You don't always need to be in the know. Keep your head down and keep moving.
- **Sprint.** Take aim at those small things that won't take much time, but just hang around to bug you. Block time and power through them.

Deep thoughts about Coco Chanel:

Coco Chanel had a strategy for being perfectly dressed for parties: "Before you leave the house, look in the mirror and remove one accessory." Apply this concept to your non-party time! Take your to-do or errand list and proactively remove one item. With the "n-1" strategy, you'll set yourself up for success and have a much less stressful day along the way. Try this at work, too!

Exercise: Remove Five Things

What five things are you doing now that you can stop doing? These could be big jobs or small.

Get Help

Closely related to the Determine chapter, here you are engaging with the VIP and others in your life to improve your life balance.

- **Engage help and expect more.** You would be surprised how capable people are, when you give them a chance.
- **Ask, don't hope.** Often, willingness is more abundant than mind-reading skills. Do not simmer. Ask for help and be specific.
- **Build a community.** Carpools and childcare trades are two lynchpins to many busy moms' lives. These and other swaps are great ways to help ease your burden.
- **Don't pretend.** If you seem like you have it all together, you might not appear to need help. (See "Engage help" above.)
- **Outsource.** If you have the means, think about what you can outsource. Cleaning, yard work, childcare, meal prep. Anything short of date night can be up for consideration.

Page from My Playbook:

We belong to a three family carpool, which can get pretty complicated. With seven busy kids in the carpool, exactly who needs a ride and when is constantly changing. We found an elegant technology solution – we use Microsoft's OneNote.

With one click on our phones, we all can see the up-to-the-minute schedule and any of us can update it real time. No more digging through email or texts, trying to figure out who you're supposed to get and hoping you aren't leaving anyone behind.

(This is *not* a shameless plug, it really has been life-changing! And I am guessing there are other sharing solutions out there.)

And I cannot resist sharing this last one.

Page from My Playbook:

Every Sunday evening we have Family Fold Fest at our house. Everyone participates. Here's how it works. I wash the laundry over the weekend, and Sunday night we dump it on the floor in the family room. Then everyone finds their own clothes in the pile, folds them, and puts them away in drawers. Ta-da! Laundry folded and put away in less than thirty minutes!

What I love about this: Division of labor, family time together (who needs Disneyland?), life skill for my kids, and guilty parties experience the consequences of multiple daily outfit changes.

I am convinced that this will be one of their favorite childhood memories. And the cool marketing name makes it a party.

To make Family Fold Fest work required three concessions from me. I had to: ask for help; let others do it their way; and lower the quality bar (and I mean *really* lower it, in the case of my son).

Exercise: What Works for You

Now it's time to pick your favorites from the chapter to try.

From the lists in this section, list five things you are going to try. Put a date by each.

What impact might these changes have?

DEFEND Your Progress

Your final step is to defend the progress you've made to improve your life balance. Once you have your life balance where you want it (or at least closer to where you want it), you want to ensure you don't lose any gains you've earned. This requires vigilance and work.

Your mindset for this chapter:
- Embrace the importance of defending your progress.
- Commit to doing it.

By the end of this chapter you will have
1. Built your flex philosophy.
2. Scheduled your defense sessions for the next twelve months.

Flex Philosophy

Your flex philosophy will determine how flexible you're willing to be with the choices you've made to create your life balance. With the realities of the modern workplace, some ability to flex is imperative. However, if you flex too often, that can be even worse than not having boundaries at all. People won't know what to expect and you will not be honoring your choices. The same dynamic is true when flexing for family and friends.

Exercise: Flex Philosophy

Use the following questions to help identify your flex philosophy.

For which VIPs are you willing to flex your life balance boundaries? Why?

For which VIPs are you unwilling to flex your life boundaries? Why not?

How will you protect your boundaries?

At a minimum, make sure you're not training your VIPs to expect you to flex for their convenience! And, when you do flex, notice how you feel later. Are you resentful? Was it worth it?

Page from My Playbook:

I had pretty clear lines to protect my life balance, but I also realized that a certain level of flexibility would serve both me and my company. To avoid tossing my boundaries out the window, I thought carefully about exceptions before agreeing. Team meetings and other one-on-one meetings – they could be scheduled during my normal working hours with rare exceptions. Meeting with executives or large groups who already have a set meeting time – for those I would flex.

My job also involved occasional travel, which tosses all boundaries out of the window. But with enough notice and planning, I made it work. (And to be honest, sometimes it was great to have time to focus *only* on work. Nearly relaxing.)

Now that you have your flex philosophy, let's look at how to defend your life balance from your... well... life.

Life Happens

Certain triggers make it obvious that your life balance will be challenged. It's hard not to notice when a newborn arrives or you get a new job.

When something of this magnitude happens, it's a great time to review your life balance, starting with your priorities and success measures. You will need to re-design your life based on your new reality. Try not to cling to what worked before if it no longer works for you. Embrace the new reality and make the best tradeoffs for you at this time to optimize your life balance.

A more insidious attack on your life balance is the drift. It's not a major upheaval, or even something you notice right away. But one day, you feel it. Stress is higher; your life feels out of control. There was no major change, just hundreds of small decisions that have upset your balanced state. Not having a flex policy can accelerate this drift.

To defend against this and avoid getting into a position of needing to fully retrain yourself and others, maintain a schedule of routine maintenance.

Routine Maintenance

Just as your car needs regular oil changes and more extensive routine maintenance to run in top shape, your life balance needs to be monitored and managed. There is no check-engine light (although high stress and fatigue are good indicators), so you'll need to create your own system.

To keep on top of the routine maintenance, create a series of Life balance defense sessions and put them on your calendar. These appointments are exclusively to focus on maintaining or improving your life balance. Just like anything important in your life that takes time, you need to commit and schedule time to do this.

Here is an initial cadence.

Subject: LIFE BALANCE DEFENSE

Weekly – 10 minutes
Review your calendar for the week ahead.
- What's going well? (Remember - celebrate!)
- Any red flags you need to address? Are you double-booked?
- Did you make time for your priorities? Are they reflected in your calendar?
- What can you delete?

Monthly – 30 minutes
Take a step back every month to monitor how well you are honoring your priorities. Ask yourself the following:

- What's going well? (Remember - celebrate!)
- Rate your stress level and life-balance satisfaction. How are you trending?
- Are you committing to too much?
- Are you asking for clarity? Are you taking your time to decide?

Watch yourself!
- Is your saboteur serving you?
- Are you feeding your perfectionist/procrastinator/hero?

Any re-training of your VIPs needed? Who?

Quarterly – 90 minutes
This is a good rhythm to go back and review your exercises.

- Are you making tradeoffs in alignment with your priorities?
- Is your flex strategy working?

- Where are you feeling the pain?
- Changes needed? Create action statements starting with "I will..."
- Progress made? Again, don't forget to celebrate.

Annually – 120 minutes

At least once a year, do the entire model over. It will go faster than the first time through, but do more than just review and approve last year's. At a minimum, complete the following exercises.

1. Balance and Stress Baseline Exercise.
   - How does your score compare to a year ago?
   - Celebration? Or time to see what's not working?

2. Priorities and Values Exercise.
   - Any significant changes from last year?
   - How well are you honoring your priorities?
   - Has your alignment improved?

3. Future Self.
   - What your future self say to you about your past year?
   - Are you on the right track?
   - What changes would s/he suggest?

Exercise: Scheduling

Put these life-balance defense sessions on your calendar now for the next twelve months (minimum). If online, use the recurring meeting function to make this easy and leave the end date open – it will schedule them in perpetuity. If on paper, do the full year.

Make these meetings with yourself a priority. For me, I think of these like I do my hair color appointments. Critical to mental health and highly prioritized.

If you need to reschedule when they get closer, do not delay them for more than a couple of days, or before you know it, another month will fly by. And reschedule – don't delete!

Wrapping Up

Anytime you read a book like this, even if you carefully complete the exercises, you won't get the true value unless you actually make the changes in your life. (Case in point, my reading thirty books on home organization didn't organize my house.)

As a reminder, what was your commitment score? _____

And one more reminder of the silver bullet.

Decide what you want, and build your life to make it true.
Make decisions and tradeoffs that best honor your life priorities.

Now, summarize your key learning for each section. Then name 1-3 things you are going to do differently to improve your life balance. Choose things you will actually do.

Design the life you want.

Diagnose where you are today.

Deal with yourself.

Determine the role of others.

Decide smarter.

Do what it takes.

Defend your progress.

Congratulations!

You've made it through *The Life Balance Playbook*!

Congratulations on committing to improving your life balance. You can do it. You deserve it.

Have successes or tips to share?

Go to www.lifebalanceplaybook.com. I would love to hear from you!

Acknowledgements

I am surrounded by an amazing tribe that has been supporting me on this journey. A special shout-out to Danielle for her innocent request which launched this project, and to my early readers Shannon and Tamie. The book is less boring because of them.

I also thank my coaches, mentors, coachees, mentees, my awesome coach community, and the many people I have worked with over my career so far. They all helped shape the content of this book through our collective experience. And also I thank everyone I told about this book who encouraged me by saying, "I need that." I hope it will be useful.

Thank you, Christina, editor extraordinaire, who not only made this book better but also helped ensure it actually got done with her direct feedback and encouraging nudges. Thanks for being flexible about my irrational dislike of semi-colons.

My family also deserves credit for motivating and supporting my quest for balance in my life. And when my kids asked me, "How's your book coming?" (which they did ... a lot), it definitely made want to complete this goal. I raise a glass to my parents, who taught me to put my family first. And finally, to my husband, who has been my partner in building our life of balance that is a daily gift.

Made in the USA
San Bernardino, CA
03 September 2015